PIANO SOLO

PIRATES of the CARIBBEAN
DEAD MAN'S CHEST

ISBN-13: 978-1-4234-1908-2
ISBN-10: 1-4234-1908-1

Disney characters and artwork © Disney Enterprises, Inc.

WALT DISNEY MUSIC COMPANY

DISTRIBUTED BY

HAL•LEONARD®
CORPORATION

7777 W. BLUEMOUND RD. P.O. BOX 13819 MILWAUKEE, WI 53213

In Australia Contact:
Hal Leonard Australia Pty. Ltd.
4 Lentara Court
Cheltenham, Victoria, 3192 Australia
Email: ausadmin@halleonard.com

Visit Hal Leonard Online at
www.halleonard.com

JACK SPARROW

Music by HANS ZIMMER

Moderately slow

(2nd time R.H. 8va)

THE KRAKEN

Music by HANS ZIMMER

Slow and steady

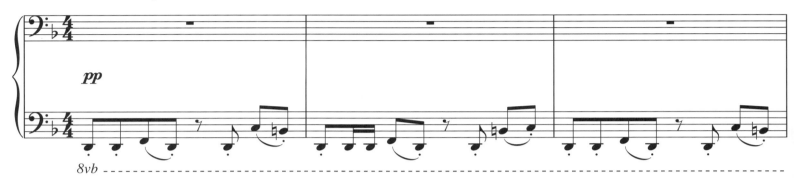

With pedal

I'VE GOT MY EYE ON YOU

Music by HANS ZIMMER

DAVY JONES

Music by HANS ZIMMER

Tempo I

Both hands 8va - - - - - - - - - - - - - - - - - -

L.H.

p

(8va) -

(8va) -

(loco)

(8va) -

DINNER IS SERVED

Music by HANS ZIMMER

Waltz tempo

TWO HORNPIPES
(Fisher's Hornpipe)

By SKIP HENDERSON

WHEEL OF FORTUNE

Music by HANS ZIMMER

Moderately fast

With pedal

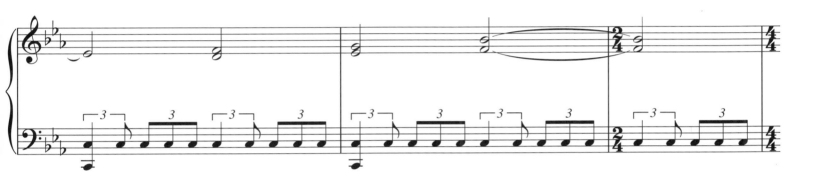

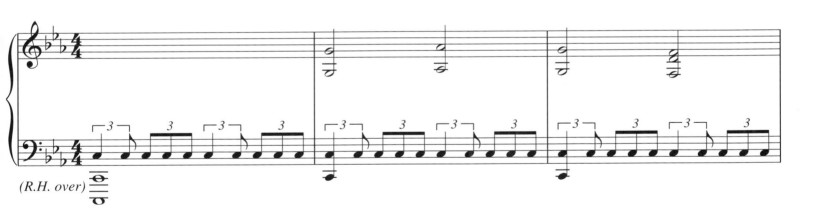

(R.H. over)

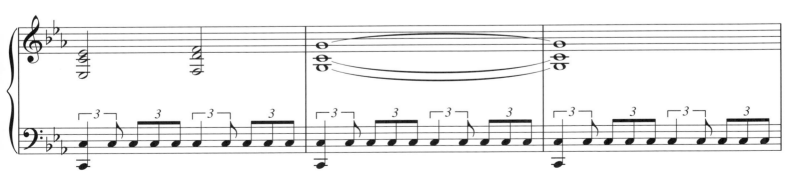

DAVY JONES PLAYS HIS ORGAN

Music by HANS ZIMMER

52